CW00493951

SINGING FOR MUSICAL THEATRE

Sight-Singing

ABRSM Grades 1–3

from 2019

Sight-singing is a skill with many benefits. It helps you perform new music with confidence and learn songs more quickly. It can be a useful skill to demonstrate in auditions and, for example, it could help you step into a new role at short notice.

These tests have been designed to be relevant to Musical Theatre singers. They are in attractive, accessible styles and include optional words. Each short piece starts with a piano introduction consisting of the final bars of the test you will then sing. The piano part either doubles (Grades 1 and 2) or closely supports (Grade 3) the melody line throughout, so you can use your listening skills to find the tune, as well as read it.

Notes

- In the exam, you will be asked to sing a different short piece of music that you have not previously seen. This sight-singing test will be accompanied by the examiner at the piano.
- The tests are printed with clear and simple words in English. You have the option to sing these or, if you prefer, to sing using any vowel (with or without consonant) or sol-fa. This choice will not affect the marking.
- In this book, separate bass-clef versions are provided for a selection of the tests. For practice purposes, you can also make your own bass-clef transpositions of the remaining treble-clef tests. In the exam, you should let the examiner know if you would prefer a bass-clef test.
- In the exam, the examiner will play the key-chord and starting note, then give a two-bar count-in before playing the piano introduction, ending with the first chord of the bar where the voice part begins. You will then be given half a minute in which to look through the music and try it out loud (unaccompanied), before you will be asked to sing it for assessment.
- At the end of the half-minute preparation time, the examiner will play the key-chord and starting note again, then give a two-bar count-in before playing the introduction for the actual test. You should join in where the voice part begins, maintaining the pulse and continuing at the same tempo as the introduction.

First published in 2018 by ABRSM (Publishing) Ltd, a wholly owned subsidiary of ABRSM

Music origination by Julia Bovee
Printed in England by Halstan & Co. Ltd, Amersham, Bucks., on materials from sustainable sources
P16015

Grade 1

1

I love Saturday

Lively
vocal range
key-chord and starting note
I love Sat-ur-day,
Sun-day too!
Work is done,
time for fun!

2

I am happy

Moderately
I am hap-py
to be me.
I'm feel-ing fine,
I'm feel-ing free!

3

Breakfast

Lively
f
Cer - e - al, toast with
mar-ma-lade too, tea for me and cof-fee for you.

4

Up, up, up

Happily
p
Up, up, up in the
sky so blue, o - ver the sea, fly - ing to you.

5 I'm like a bird

Cheerfully
p
I'm like a bird that
p leggiero
sings all day, I want the world to hear what I say.
f
f

6 Soon we'll be home

Hopefully
p
Soon we'll be home,
p
soon we'll be home. Give me your hand and soon we'll be home.
f
f

7 (𝄞)

Knowing you

Thoughtfully
p
Know - ing you I've
p
come to find,
f
friends like you are one of a kind.
f

7 (𝄢)

Knowing you

Thoughtfully
p
Know - ing you I've
p
come to find,
f
friends like you are one of a kind.
f

8 (𝄞) When I look in your eyes

Sweetly
p
When I look in your eyes so blue,
f
I for - get ev -'ry - one but you.

8 (𝄢) When I look in your eyes

Sweetly
p
When I look in your eyes so blue,
f
I for - get ev -'ry - one but you.

9 (𝄞)

Look how the stars

Gently
Look how the stars
shine in the sky, blink as the moon catch-es your eye.

9 (𝄢)

Look how the stars

Gently
Look how the stars
shine in the sky, blink as the moon catch-es your eye.

10 (𝄞) Don't look back

Slowly
p
Don't look back,
p
yes - ter - day's gone.
f
Keep mov - ing on and on.
f

10 (𝄢) Don't look back

Slowly
p
Don't look back,
p
yes - ter - day's gone.
f
Keep mov - ing on and on.
f

Grade 2

1 Look at me

vocal range
key-chord and starting note
Tenderly
p
Look at me, and you'll see I'm here to stay, I will help you.

2 Turn to the left

Moderately
mf
mf leggiero
Turn to the left or turn to the right? Don't know which way to go.
p

3 I see a crocodile

Lively
mp
I see a cro-co-dile
mp
look-ing at me,
f
think he's plan-ning to have me for tea!
f

4 Happy Ending

Happily
mf
I love a hap-py
mf
end-ing!
f
Hap-py and fun-ny too.
f

5 Lucky star

Hopefully
mp
Luck-y star, shin-ing bright,
mp
shine your light on me, shine your light on all you see.
f
f

6 In this box

Thoughtfully
f
In this box is my
f
mp
sis - ter's watch, Grand - pa got it for her birth - day.
mp

7 (𝄞)

When you see the moon

Dreamily
mp
When you see the moon and
stars in the sky,
mf
then you know it's time to say good - night.
mp
mf

7 (𝄢)

When you see the moon

Dreamily
mp
When you see the moon and
stars in the sky,
mf
then you know it's time to say good - night.
mp
mf

8 (𝄞) Some things are red

Thoughtfully
mp
Some things are red, and
some things are green.
mf
Some things are black and white, or
p
so it seems.

8 (𝄢) Some things are red

Thoughtfully
mp
Some things are red, and
some things are green.
mf
Some things are black and white, or
p
so it seems.

9 (𝄞)

Golden rays

Warmly
p
Gold - en rays of gold-en
p
sun - shine,
mf
warm my face as I dream.
mf

9 (𝄢)

Golden rays

Warmly
p
Gold - en rays of gold-en
p
sun - shine,
mf
warm my face as I dream.
mf

10 (𝄞)

River so wide

Flowing
mf
Riv - er so wide, where
mf
do you lead? Flow - ing so end - less - ly.
p
p

10 (𝄢)

River so wide

Flowing
mf
Riv - er so wide, where
mf
do you lead? Flow - ing so end - less - ly.
p
p

Grade 3

1 Here's a song

Lively
vocal range
key-chord and starting note
f
Here's a song for to - day, here's a song from the past.
mp
f
Here's a song that we love to sing and here's a song that will last.

2 I love to sail

Flowing
mf
mf
I love to sail on a warm af - ter - noon,
rall.
p
on - ly re - turn - ing by the light of the moon.
p

3

Deep in the darkest wood

Thoughtfully
p
p
Deep in the dark-est wood where the trees meet a-bove your head,
mf
none of the clear blue sky breaks through, so I have heard it said.
mf

4 Way up high

Happily
mf
mf
Way up high on the moun-tain-side, you can hear me sing my song.
rall.
f
That's where I feel_ most a - live, that's where I be - long!
f

5

I'm a child of the city

With a rock feel
f
I'm a child of the city, child of the city, how I love cit - y nights.
mf
f
When I'm far from the cit - y, how I long to see the cit - y lights.

6 I hear the gentle breeze

Flowing
mp
mp
I hear the gen-tle breeze sing to me. It tells of things that I long to see,
mf
rall.
f
far - a-way pla - ces beau-ti - ful lands o - ver the sands.
mf
f

7 (𝄞)

Fly little robin

Bouncy
mf
Fly lit - tle rob - in
touch the sky,
p
spread your wings,
fly right by.
mf
Fly lit - tle rob - in
high and low,
f
you have far to go.

7 Fly little robin

Bouncy
mf
Fly lit - tle rob - in
mf
touch the sky,
p
spread your wings,
fly right by.
p
mf
Fly lit - tle rob - in high and low,
f
you have far to go.
mf
f

8 (𝄞)

Evil Spell

Spookily
f
Eye of newt, toe-nail of a frog,
f leggiero
now stir it ve - ry well.
p
Dou - ble, dou - ble,
p
toil and trou - ble, here's an e - vil spell!
f
f

8 (𝄢) Evil Spell

Spookily
f
Eye of newt, toe-nail of a frog,
f leggiero
now stir it ve - ry well.
p
Dou - ble, dou - ble,
toil and trou - ble, here's an e - vil spell!
f

9

I'll Be Calling You

Lively rock
mp
Some-time soon, when
mp
I get home a-gain, I'll be call-ing you.
f
Just a day or two, I'll be call-ing you.
f

9 (𝄢) I'll Be Calling You

Lively rock
mp
Some-time soon, when
mp
I get home a-gain, I'll be call-ing you.
f
Just a day or two, I'll be call-ing you.
f

10 (𝄞)

Trying to get back

Sadly
p
p
mf
p
Try - ing to get back to where_ I be - long, I'm
mf
p
lost and I'm feel - ing so far from home.

10 Trying to get back

Sadly
p
mf
p
Try - ing to get back to where_ I be - long, I'm
mf
p
lost and I'm feel - ing so far from home.

11

Down on the beach

Brightly
f
Down on the beach the sand is fine,
down on the beach the sun does shine.
mf
Out in the sea,
catch-ing the waves,
f
I love my ho - li - day beach time!

11 (𝄢)

Down on the beach

Brightly
f
Down on the beach the sand is fine,
down on the beach the sun does shine.
mf
Out in the sea,
catch-ing the waves,
I love my ho - li - day beach time!